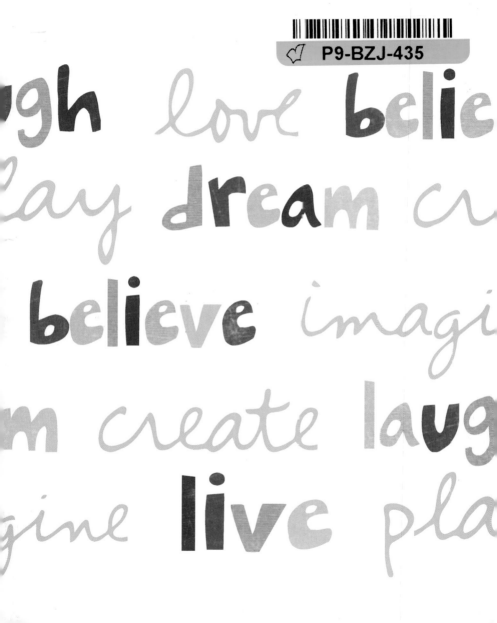

Sandra Magsamen is a best-selling and award-winning artist, author, and designer whose meaningful and message-driven art has touched millions of lives, one heart at a time. She lives happily and artfully in Vermont with her family and their dog, Olive.

A big thank-you to my amazing studio team of Hannah Barry and Karen Botti. Their creativity and spirit have been a gift.

Sandra Magsamen

Text and illustrations © 2016 Hanny Girl Productions, Inc. www.sandramagsamen.com
Exclusively represented by Mixed Media Group, Inc. NY, NY
Cover and internal design © 2016 by Sandra Magsamen

Published by Sourcebooks, Inc.
P.O. Box 4410, Naperville, Illinois 60567-4410
(630) 961-3900
Fax: (630) 961-2168
www.sourcebooks.com

Printed and bound in China.
LEO 10 9 8 7 6 5 4 3 2 1

make every day count

wise and uplifting ways to inspire your days

Sandra Magsamen

§ sourcebooks

Every day is a new opportunity to follow your heart, to dream big, to play, to reach for the stars, to celebrate life and to create the life you imagine.

This gift book artfully offers heartfelt inspiration, some friendly advice, a little nudging and a dash of courage to help you make every day count!

Sandra Magsamen

follow your heart

Follow your heart, live passionately **and** embrace each day as if it were the last! Following your heart means to listen, to feel and to act consciously and enthusiastically with your focus on what only you can bring to this world. Push self-doubt out of the way and go for it! Life is precious. Each heartbeat is a gift. Live with an open heart and allow care, compassion, empathy, understanding, forgiveness, generosity and kindness to guide your decisions, actions and life.

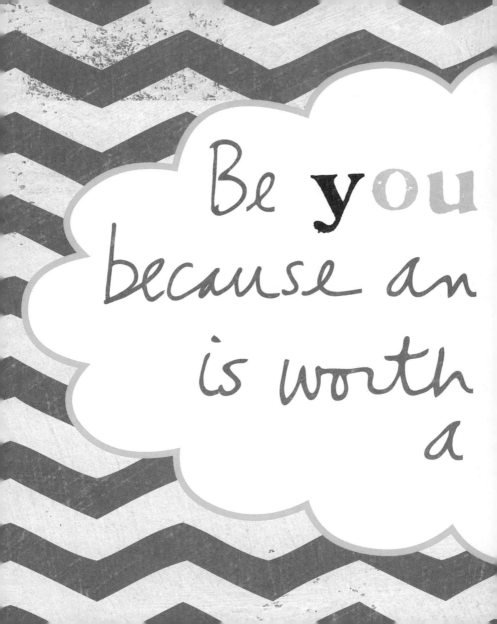

rself,
original
more than
copy.

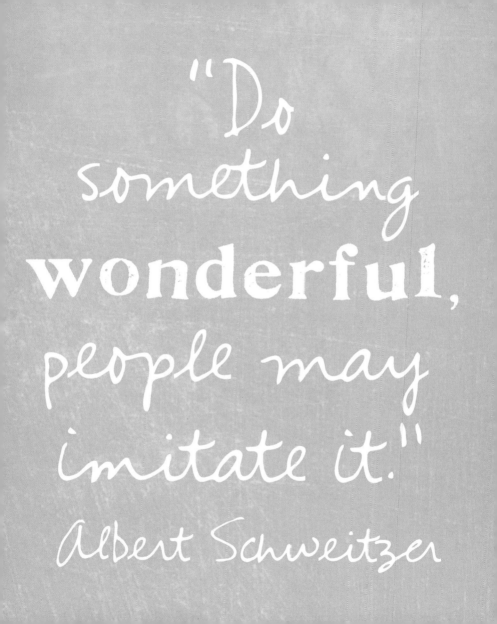

"What if

Oh, but

what if

Erin

I fall? darling, you **fly?**"
Hanson

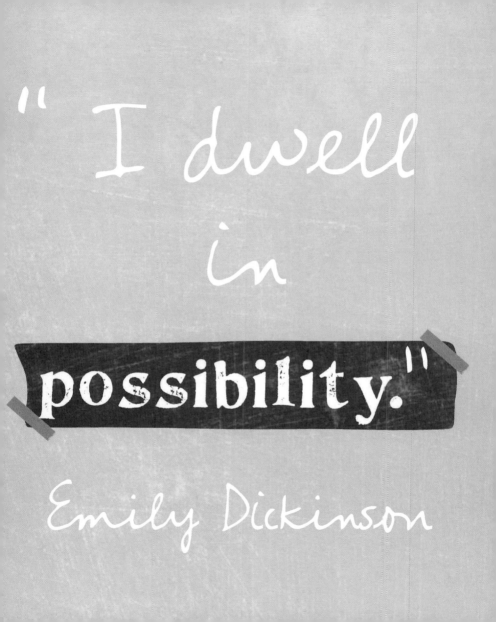

"Just don't give
what you really
there is **love**
I don't think you
Ella

up trying to do
want to do. Where
and **inspiration**,
can go wrong."
Fitzgerald

Our *dreams* are powerful—
perhaps the most powerful thing
we have in this world.
The *dreams* we dream are at
the heart of our goals,
desires and ambitions.
Ultimately, our *dreams*
guide the actions and decisions
we make in life. *Dreams* are
like little compasses inside
our minds and hearts, directing
us toward that place we long for.
Honor your *dreams*, act on them,
dream big and your
dreams will come true.

When life
knocks
you down,
roll over
and look at
the **stars.**

your
one can
but you.

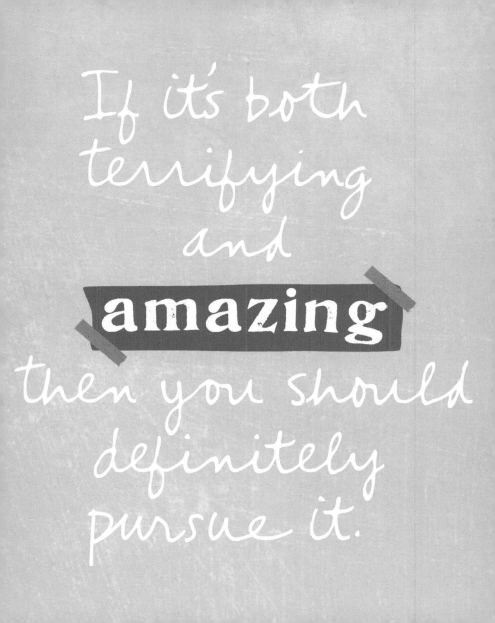

Turn

into

and

into

"can't"
"can"
dreams
plans.

All too often, we are informed at a young age to grow up and stop playing. We are encouraged to attend to our life in a serious way and leave the playing behind us. Most of us take this nudging and advice to heart and abandon our playful selves, believing this path is the way to a successful and happy life. Well, it turns out that we might have been a bit shortsighted. Research shows that play is at the heart of a happy life. Play rejuvenates and revitalizes, it helps you see the world from different points of view, it rekindles your optimism, encourages experimentation, invites laughter and is all around just plain fun. So, play more, smile more, laugh more, invent stuff, try new things, make mistakes and be goofy 'cause it is all this play that rejuvenates us, freshens our minds and makes life joyful.

The only you need "**bags**" and

"bs"
today is
"shoes"!

Always wear your invisible **crown.**

happy
others look
they become
py
contagious!

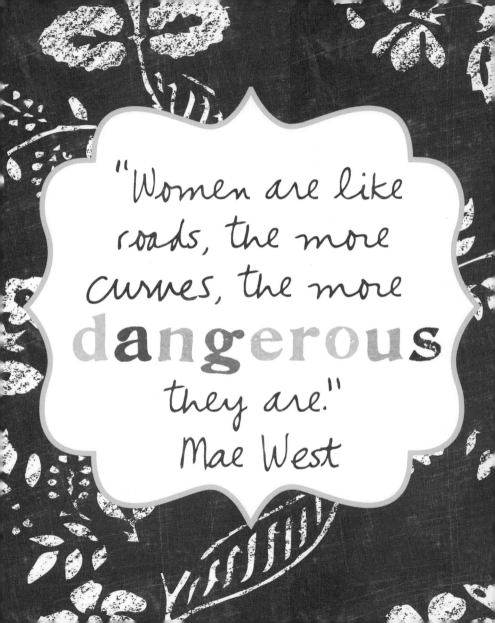

you want,
something
to regret
morning...
late.

In order to be successful in life, you must become your own biggest fan, your best cheerleader and the president of your own fan club. When the rest of the world doubts and questions your thoughts and convictions, it is a strong belief in yourself that will carry you through. No mountain is too high and no challenge is too great if you truly believe in yourself. Remember, you must never, ever, ever give up. Keep striving and reaching for those dreams and you'll surely find yourself among the brightest and most *beautiful stars.*

rains, look **bows.** dark, **stars.**

Never stop
exploring,
'cause life
would be
boring!

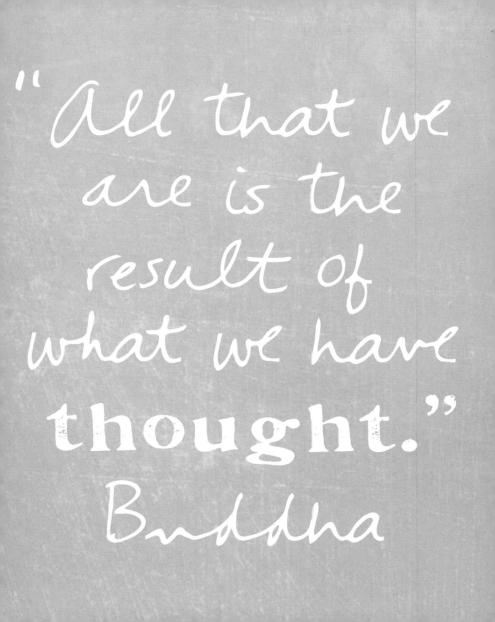

lose...
either
or
learn.

We often become so caught up in the hustle and bustle of our everyday lives that it is easy to forget how lucky we are to simply be! It's pretty amazing, isn't it? This world we live in? The fact that we have air in our lungs, brains that think wonderful thoughts, hearts that beat and love? What about the purple mountain majesties, the rainbows with tons of colors, the smiles on people's faces, the giggles from kids being tickled, the snow falling like lace and so much more?

Celebrate it!

Live the you love the you

No one ever injured their eyesight by looking on the **bright side.**

isn't
on the
side,
where you
it.

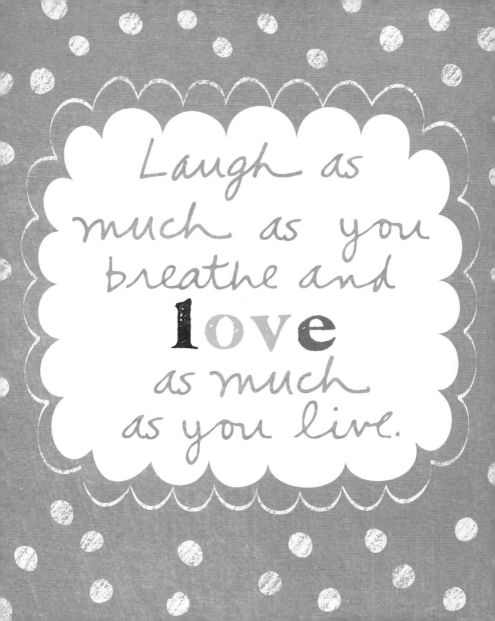

The sign of a **beautiful** person is that they always see beauty in others.

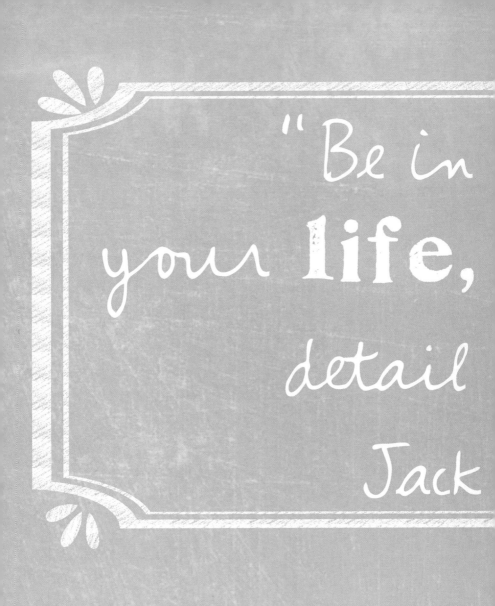

"Be in your **life,** detail Jack

love with
every
of it."
Kerouac

We are the artists of our lives and we can *create the life we imagine.* The secret to creating the life we desire is in imagining, seeing and knowing what we really want. Ask yourself lots of questions, like, "How do I want to live?" "How do I want to connect with the people I love?" "What kind of job do I covet?" "Where do I feel the happiest?" and "What does my ideal life look like?" Once you imagine and clearly see what you want to create, get started. Bit by bit and day by day, do the work to create what is in your heart, and like a work of art, you will begin to see your life take shape.

The happiest **have** the everything, the of

people don't
best of
they **make**
best
everything.

The best way
to predict
your future
is to
create it.

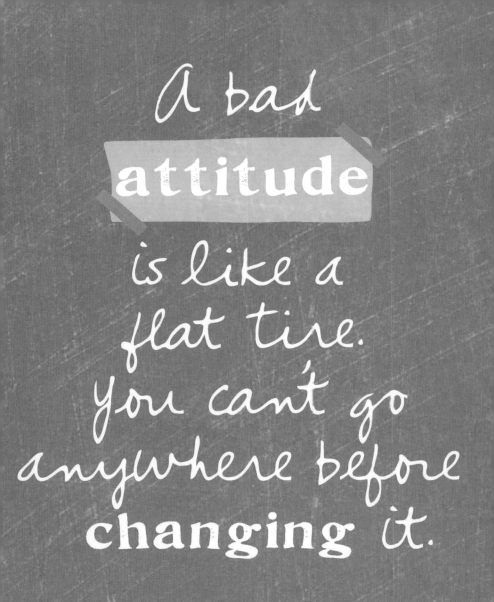

"There are flowers for want Henri

always
those who
to see them."

Matisse

FLY GUY'S AMAZING TRICKS

Tedd Arnold

Cartwheel Books

An Imprint of Scholastic Inc.

For Ava and Jack

Library of Congress Cataloging-in-Publication Data

Arnold, Tedd, author.
Fly Guy's amazing tricks / Tedd Arnold. —First edition.
pages cm. — (Fly Guy ; 14)
Summary: Fly Guy has learned a lot of new tricks, but when he shows off at dinner time
he and Buzz get into trouble—though later they prove useful.
ISBN 978-0-545-76926-6
1. Flies—Juvenile fiction. 2. Tricks—Juvenile fiction. 3. Friendship—Juvenile fiction. [1. Flies—Fiction.
2. Tricks—Fiction. 3. Friendship—Fiction.] I. Title. II. Series: Arnold, Tedd. Fly Guy ; #14.

PZ7.A7379Fo 2014
813.54—dc23

2013051319

12 11 10 9 8 7 6 5 4 3 2 1   14 15 16 17 18

Printed in China 38
This edition first printing, September 2014

A boy had a pet fly.
He named him Fly Guy.
And Fly Guy could
say the boy's name—

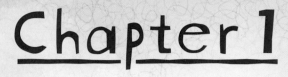

Chapter 1

Buzz's friends came to see
The Amazing Fly Guy Circus.

Buzz said, "Get ready for Fly Guy's amazing new tricks!"

"Now," said Buzz,
"The Backstroke!"

"And now," said Buzz,
"The Big Booger!"

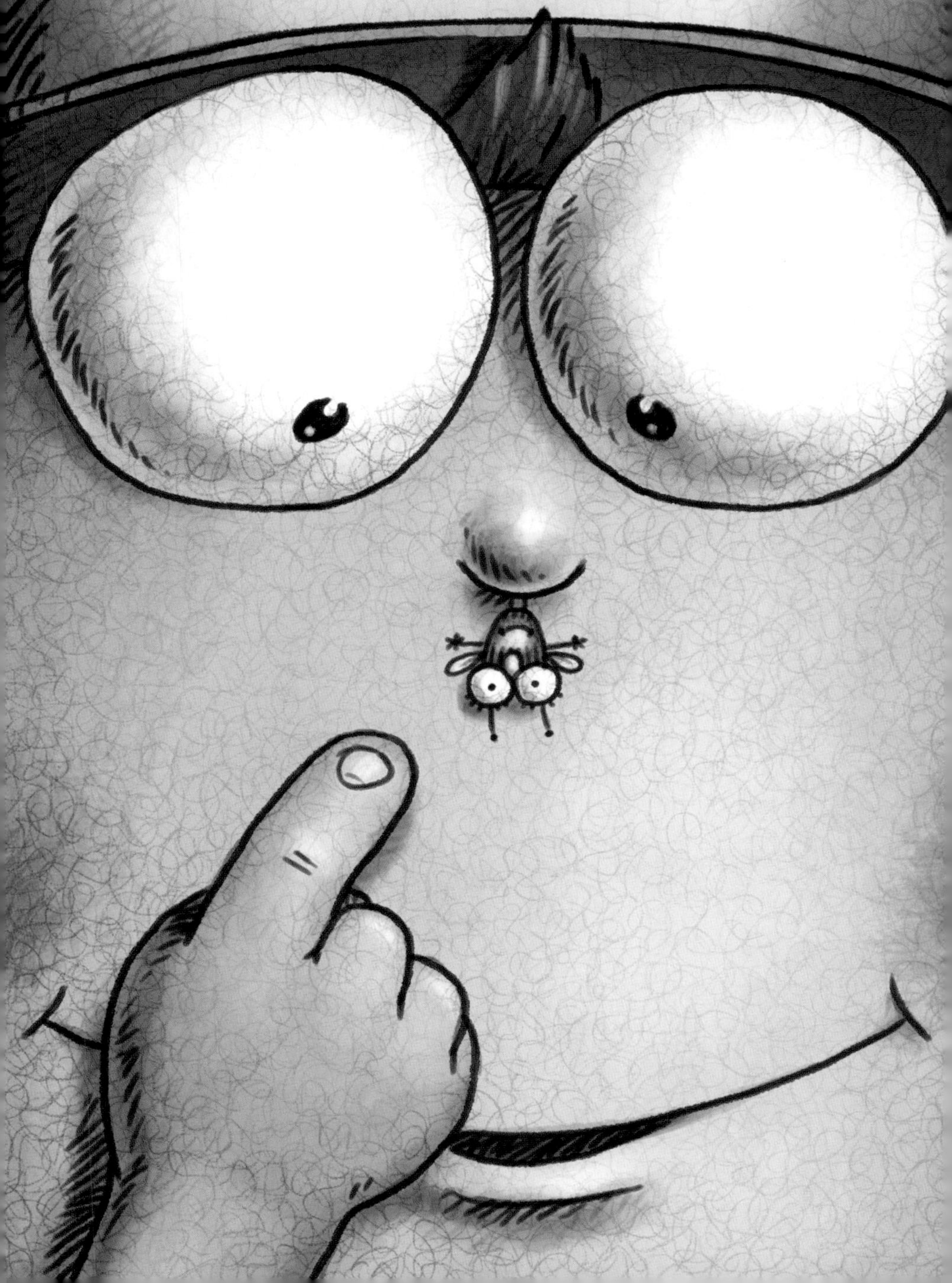

"Time for supper," said
Mom. Buzz's friends all
went home.

Chapter 2

At the dinner table, Buzz said, "Fly Guy learned new tricks."

Fly Guy did The Backstroke in Mom's milk.

Buzz cried, "Stop, Fly Guy!"
But Fly Guy didn't hear him.

Fly Guy did The Dizzy
Doozie around Dad's head.

Buzz cried, "Stop, Fly Guy!"
But Fly Guy didn't hear him.

Fly Guy did The Big Booger.
Buzz caught him.

"Stop, Fly Guy!" he said.
"Let's clean up this mess."

Chapter 3

Outside, Buzz said to Fly Guy, "I have an idea. Do your tricks only when you hear the word NOW."

YEZZ

A big kid walked by.
He laughed. "Are you
talking to a bug?"
Buzz didn't answer.

The kid said, "Do you have bug brains?" Buzz didn't answer.

The kid said, "Bug got your tongue?" Buzz didn't answer.

Fly Guy heard the word "NOW!"

Then Fly Guy did
The Dizzy Doozie.

And then Fly Guy did
The Big Booger.

He bumped into a garbage can.

A zillion angry flies chased
the big kid away.

Buzz said, "Fly Guy, here's a new trick for you."

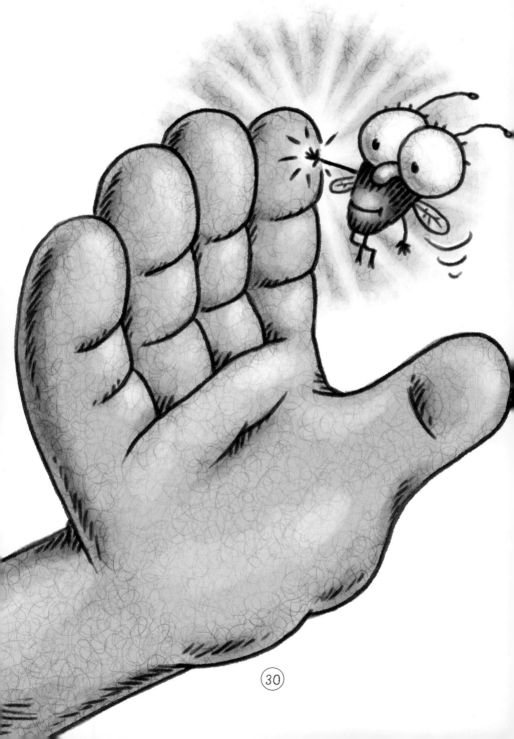